A literary critic's view of
COUSIN BELLA – THE WHORE OF MINSK

With his playwright's precise ear for the nuance of the spoken word and a novelist's gift for the colors, smells, and sensations of another era, of the things of the world as they actually were, Sherman Yellen has created a small masterpiece in a memoir called, wonderfully, Cousin Bella, the Whore of Minsk.

Startlingly funny in its frankness ("That big mouth of hers could suck a regiment dry"), Yellen's courageous, beautiful-ugly whore, his indomitable iron-tough grandmother who saves her, her adoring simple-hearted husband who protects her, the child she steals, worships and raises, the story that resolves itself in a catastrophe fit for melodrama (in fact, these true events made it to the stage of New York's Yiddish Theater), Yellen has given us the Jewish-American immigrant experience more vitally and persuasively than any writer since Isaac Bashevis Singer:

"You want trees?" Bella asks of those who leave the worn-out Lower East Side for the greener pastures of Flatbush and the Bronx, "go back to Russia"... Who needed nature. Nature was for the goyim.*

*Christopher Davis, novelist and critic, Senior Lecturer in the Arts emeritus from Bryn Mawr College, winner of the O'Henry Prize, author of eleven novels, nominee for the National Book Award, and author of several studies of world literature.

Cousin Bella –
The Whore of Minsk

and

A Christmas Lilly

Sherman Yellen

MORECLACKE PUBLISHING
New York City

For information, contact Moreclacke Publishing at
info@moreclacke.com or
325 West 45th Street, Suite 609, New York, NY 10036

Graphic design by Robert Armin

Audiobook available from Audible.com and iTunes

First Printing

LCCN: 2014903631

ISBN-10: 1495290433

ISBN-13: 978-1495290435

Published in the United States of America

For my late sister Simone –
who was my co-conspirator in our shared childhood

PROLOGUE
BEFORE THE CURTAIN RISES

Sometime in the early 1970s, my Cousin Bella, an elderly relative of my mother's, asked to meet with me saying, "I got a life to tell." I winced. As a writer, I find most lives interesting but few can sort out the beguiling from the boring in their own experience. And I feared that this was about to be an afternoon of the relentlessly tedious – a story of a drab life sewed together stitch by mind-numbing stitch by this former seamstress, a plain-looking old woman who might be cast in a film's crowd scene of arrivals at Ellis Island, but never as a leading lady, not even as a featured player. Nevertheless, I accepted Cousin Bella's invitation to meet and listen to the story of her life. She had been kind to me when I was a young boy; alone among my relatives she never asked that deadly question of a child, "So how is school?"

I knew that she was an immigrant from Czarist Russia who had spent her adult years on the Lower

East Side of Manhattan, long married to a furniture salesman, silent Cousin Max; a childless woman earning her living making slipcovers for other people's sofas in the Bronx and Brooklyn. Was she going to tell me that she had once shoplifted a lipstick from a Woolworth's? Or that she had had an affair with a kosher butcher to relieve the boredom of her days with her silent husband of fifty years? None of this felt promising to the busy, impatient forty-year-old man that I was – a writer of screenplays and librettos for musical theater.

And so I sat and listened as family duty turned to fascination, taking notes as she told me about her life. I kept telling myself "This can't be. No. This doesn't happen to people I know. Not to people from my family. Certainly not to people who look like Bella." Here was a life with enough hardship, crime, deception and desperation to fill two Dostoyevsky novels.

After Cousin Bella was done speaking about her past – one that she recalled with precise, enviable detail – I thanked her and assured her that I would get around to writing it as soon as I had the time. My first thought was that this was the most fascinating *bubbemyseh* (Yiddish for a grandmother's tale) – and often an incredible one – that I had ever heard. So I called my mother – a woman who worshipped at the altar of truth – and went over the details of this most remarkable story. When Bella's story was confirmed by my mother, and then reconfirmed by my cousin Serena, who had heard it all from her own father, my Uncle Frank, I put my notes away for "later." Later is too often a synonym for never. Then, suddenly, with the blink of an eye (otherwise known as the passage of forty years), I was no longer the young relative listening to an old woman's story but a man as old as, if not older, than Bella was when she recounted her life to me, and I now understood that need to have her story told – to have one's life with all its passion and its pain rescued from oblivion through the magic act of words. And so I feel relief that, at last, I have kept a long delayed promise. All of us want to leave a record of our lives for future generations. Not many of us make it out of the high school yearbook into the history books, but everyone has a story to tell, although few have lived lives with the heartbreak and the strength to survive shown by my remarkable cousin Bella.

If Bella's story reads like a melodrama, melodrama was the way of life for many of the turn of the 20th Century Eastern European Jews. They had fled persecution in the old world only to find poverty and hardship in the new world. When they arrived they often became the victims of chance and the improbable was the probable – the very nature of melodrama. Is it any wonder that Yiddish theater flourished on melodramas that were so close to the lives of its audience? Cousin Bella is long dead, so I could not go over her story once again detail by detail, relying on my notes and memory to tell her story.

What was remarkable to me then, and what I recalled as I wrote this piece, was that Bella did not present herself as a victim of her own life, but one who was, for good or ill, the maker of it.

I am fortunate in my memory of my childhood. While some are left with fleeting impressions of their own past, I have detailed engravings of my own, as in *A Christmas Lilly*. The events of Bella's story are true, not family folklore, and if I have filled in the dots from time to time with lines that connect these events, I did so believing that they were lines that were pure Cousin Bella as I remember her. But is it absolutely accurate? Stephen Blair, a classicist at Princeton University wrote best about accuracy in a recent *New Yorker* letter: "…no historical account can entirely mirror reality… a historian must prioritize clarity over chronology, emphasize casual connections, and suppress irrelevancies. Even an unbiased historian, privy to flawless information, will compose a story that, though it may be inspired by a particular event, isn't a true account of it." That does not mean that Cousin Bella's tale is a fiction. I can attest to its fundamental truth. But in writing it I felt less an historian than an archeologist who reconstructed the fragments of a life that I was obliged to paste together in order to view it as a whole. Since the events of the story began shortly before the turn of the 20th Century, decades before my own birth, I was not a witness to the events Bella told to me, but rather the heir to her story.

As an addendum to Cousin Bella's story, perhaps I should mention that, with two Aunt Idas in the family, one of whom plays a featured role in my own memoir tale *A Christmas Lilly*, also included in this book, I took the liberty of changing my old cousin Ida's name to Bella to provide her with her own unique literary identity and to avoid confusion with the other Idas in my more complete family history. Since Bella means "beautiful," I trust that my otherwise homely old cousin would be flattered by the name change. Indeed, looking at her old photograph recently I found a certain strength and beauty in her face that I had never noticed before. *A Christmas Lilly*, unlike Bella's tale, is not relayed second hand but is a telling of my own experience.

One final word before the curtain rises on *Cousin Bella*. I would not have published this book without the encouragement of Robert Armin: novelist, actor, director, publisher, and friend, whose splendid audio books of *Cousin Bella* and *A Christmas Lilly* are available from Amazon, Audible and iTunes. It was Armin who pointed out certain inconsistences which prompted me to revise this edition of *Cousin Bella*, making it a more accurate version of the story previously released in my Amazon eBook.

Cousin Bella –
The Whore of Minsk

Cousin Bella, Simone and me

I

Sitting on top of a file in my office is a fading photograph of myself as a squirming one year old held in the arms of my homely, middle aged "Cousin" Bella, while my five year old sister Simone, all dark ringlets, and gorgeous in her discontent, squints into the sunlight in front of the Bronx house where we lived. The year is 1933; the place, a red brick two-story colonial building with a wide expanse of lawn that covered half the city block, the flagship building of a street that was later filled with narrow, two story brick houses. Later I was to learn that our rented house was the house that Dutch Schultz built, his unused retreat from gangland killings, situated on top of a steep hill from which no one could surprise him from above, when Andrews Avenue was still the countryside in the late twenties. My parents rented the house from an ad in *The Bronx Home News* unaware, at the time, of the real owner. It was part of their effort to secure us against the dangers of the world outside. And danger lurked everywhere.

Born in 1932, in the very same week as the Lindbergh baby kidnapping, it is no wonder that I lived under vigilant eyes. Cousin Bella had come to visit us from her tenement apartment on Rivington Street on the Lower East Side. She would arrive with needle, thread, scissors, and bolts of flowered chintz to make the ill-fitting slipcovers that would cover the rose brocade of our Sheraton style living room. It was her belief that everything in life and furniture should be concealed and allow for a little shrinkage. Perhaps that is why her story seemed so large, to allow for the shrinkage that might take place over time. Some parts of her story came to me through my mother's childhood recollections that I trusted implicitly, since mother for all her virtues and charm had no imagination. Other parts of the story come from Cousin Bella's own account during our last meeting in the early nineteen seventies shortly before her death.

I had by then written the libretto for a Broadway musical, *The Rothschilds*, and by doing that I had earned her trust as a family scribe. Who better than the infant Sherman whom she had once coddled and nurtured to tell her story? I was now a professional who lived by my wits, something she honored and trusted – more important, I was her youngest living relative – the grandson of the woman who had rescued her; and most remarkably, rescued her without judging her. She came to me that day more as a friend – despite the great difference in our ages and experience – for I had always been drawn to her and she knew it. Her visits to our house during my early childhood always excited my interest because I could tell from my mother's pleasant but reserved attitude towards Cousin Bella that there was a whiff of disapproval in the way mother looked at her. That separated Bella from all the other relatives whom my mother accepted without judgment. It was clear that my mother loved her, how often she would refer to her with sympathy as "Poor Bella" – but it was a love tempered by suspicion.

Bella was no grandmother figure; this homely, tobacco stained woman with the iron gray bun who looked years older than her age, and who treated my sister and me as conspirators in a plot we could not fathom. It was clear to me that she loved children but that she did her best to conceal it. When I was a small boy, she waited for my mother to leave the room to let me try the scissors she carried in her workbasket, since my cautious mother would have found them too sharp for the hands of a five year old. Alone together as I watched Bella cut fabrics and take measurements, she was the first and only one to let me strike a match

Simone and me at the
Andrews Avenue house

from the small wooden box she carried in her large black handbag, so that my excited hands could light her cigarette. The first match you strike is one of life's transforming moments; one has made fire and survived, so whenever I light the fire in my fireplace these days I think of my old Cousin Bella. Another time when my mother was preparing dinner out of sight and Bella was making us a new slipcover for the sofa, I remarked that I thought it wonderful that she could keep so many pins in her mouth without swallowing them. She shrugged and proceeded to teach me how, filling my mouth with the small straight pins and instructing me to press down hard with my upper lip, and squeeze my eyes half shut, constricting the muscles in my cheeks. As soon as we heard my mother approaching, I hurriedly spat out the pins into Bella's open palm. And Bella laughed conspiratorially in her deep, smoke darkened voice.

Once, a few years later when she took me to the local movie theatre, the Park Plaza, and we sat upstairs in the smoking balcony, she offered me, a ten year old, a drag on her cigarette. Since we both had suffered from asthma, she assured me that cigarettes could open up the bronchial tubes, and that her perpetual coughing was a sign that she was clearing out her lungs. These events viewed from today's perspective, might make her appear a danger to a small child, but in her own time I can assure you that Cousin Bella, pins, scissors, and cigarettes, was a saving grace in a long childhood.

As I grew a bit older, maybe twelve or thirteen, all I knew about her was that she had lived a hard life – for so our mother told us – but unlike most relatives with a history of old world poverty or illness, subjects so boring to the young that one closed one's ears to them automatically, she never spoke of her past in order to boast of having survived it, or remarked on how lucky we were, never asking us to count our blessings, an arithmetic no child can ever learn, and her restraint made her appear to live more in the present than other old relatives, the only place that children can inhabit comfortably. Alone among our relatives she did not parrot the pieties that most of the Aunts spouted and that children immediately recognize as fakery. She made no claims to virtue, so rare and so endearing to my older sister, and to me, both of us often overwhelmed by family claims of goodness that we knew we had not inherited.

Most remarkable to me was that she owned a pair of pure-bred cocker spaniels with silken ears – a fancy breed for a poor woman to have for in that era the poor did not keep dogs; perhaps a cat but never a dog. Dogs had been used in pogroms to sniff out and hunt Jews in hiding. It took years of assimilation before they were considered companionable creatures. Cousin Bella knew better than to bring her dogs with her to family occasions, but she would often show me their photographs and I found them beautiful. As far as I then knew she had no children, so the dogs were her progeny.

Now that I was a grown man Cousin Bella was ready to tell her story to me, to be relieved of its awful burden of deceit, obsession, passion and disillusion, a burden that she had carried with her for over eighty years. She held out a large yellow lined pad and a freshly sharpened pencil and advised me to take notes so that "you don't forget all about me later." I never forgot.

Bella Busch was my maternal grandmother's niece, born outside of Minsk in Belarus, Russia, to Yetta Busch and my grandmother's older brother, Abram. Bella's mother had died of typhus at the turn of the century, and Abram, Bella's father, quickly remarried to find a cook for his home and a mother for his daughter, choosing another Yetta, in the hope that this second Yetta would prove as loving as the first. This new Yetta, twice a widow, never took to the girl, but as long as her husband lived she concealed her

Simone and me

antipathy for the child, and she treated Bella with a cold but proper civility. She fed her, clothed her, and slapped her as required by the unwritten laws of step-motherhood. Bella was fifteen when her father died, and the girl was now in the sole charge of that forbidding Yetta Soloway, who dropped all pretense of caring for the child and openly revealed her implacable hatred for her.

Yetta had come to the marriage with two young sons, two stout and healthy boys, and she searched for a way to rid herself of this homely, hungry, burdensome creature who ate the leftovers that might have been used for the next day's meal. Yetta spoke to the local matchmakers, but they demanded a substantial fee for finding a mate for such a plain girl with no dowry. "You need a blind widower," one stated, "and they don't come up so often."

The stepmother reproached the girl for her ugliness, claiming that it was a deliberate act of spite and that every day Bella contrived to grow more ugly – that Bella had willed that bulbous nose and those close-set eyes that swam like tiny minnows behind her thick glasses. "Your mother, poor soul, really died by looking at you," she told the girl as a matter of fact. "And I'm not going to let you do me in. No, Bella Busch, you will not kill me before my time." Strange, but Cousin Bella had no compunction about telling me this – she saw no disgrace in being called out for her ugliness; for her the disgrace belonged to Yetta, her stepmother, who showed no mercy for a young girl in her care.

Less than a year after Bella's father Abram's death, Yetta sold her charge to Anna Bolotnikov, the local Madam in Minsk whose spacious wooden house sheltered a dozen women who served the pressing sexual needs of the local Cossacks and the town's bachelor Jews. Yetta would claim that she had merely placed Bella in the brothel as a maid. "Who would believe that one would end up as a whore? Uglier, they don't get! Who knew?" Well, in time somebody did, and that somebody was my maternal grandmother Sarah.

My grandmother, Sarah Busch Horowitz, was a small woman with a hard bony face and the blazing black eyes of the religious fanatic or the tubercular. The truth was she had little interest in religion and referred to her more observant neighbors as synagogue sinners, claiming that they used their show of piety to cover their daily peccadilloes. She was indeed tubercular and a fanatic, but her fanaticism was all in the service of her family. She had already given birth to four children, the oldest, Sam, the youngest, a toddler named Libby, later to be my mother, the remarkable and dangerously beautiful Lillian. Sarah was waiting to join her husband, who had settled in New York and was working to make the passage money to send for his family. But he had not been fortunate in the new world where he worked a pushcart among thousands of others, selling needles, threads and notions on Essex Street, occasionally picking up day jobs painting, welding rivets and repairing the Brooklyn Bridge. He was a sometimes tailor in a universe of sometimes tailors, barely making enough to rent his room, eat his meager meals, with nothing remaining to send back to his family in Russia that could pay for their passage. His sister, Maryasha, the first to immigrate, had promised to provide the passage money for his family when her dressmaking business was established, a pledge she would keep in time. My grandfather's shame was that he had left a decent upholstery business in Russia to come to America and fail. Strong, handsome, with a powerful body, he did not know what to do with his failure but be shocked by it and try to cover it up in his letters to his wife, letters that she was clever enough to disbelieve but loving enough to forgive.

Sarah lived in a village bordering the larger town of Minsk. When she visited Minsk to make a delivery

Grandmother Sarah

for the home-based upholstery business, she decided to visit her niece, Bella, at the Soloway cabin on the other side of town.

A nervous Yetta Soloway told my grandmother that young Bella had been sent off to America to work as a seamstress months before. My grandmother was at once suspicious; surely Bella would have come to say goodbye to her only living blood relative, but this sudden immigration was such a common event it could just about pass scrutiny. Yetta was nothing if not plausible. News of Bella's true whereabouts came to Sarah from a friend in Minsk when Sarah mentioned to her that Little Bella was in New York. "New York? Are you crazy?" the friend queried. "She's working as a whore in a brothel in Minsk."

Sarah approached Yetta Soloway again, who repeated her now well-rehearsed speech about sending little Bella off to America where she was boarding with a respectable Jewish family and happily engaged sewing buttons in a blouse factory. When she asked to be shown some proof of this claim, such as a letter from Bella in America, Yetta replied, "The child is a terrible ingrate. You'd think she would have sent me some money to pay back her passage – if not that, at the very least a letter to reassure me that she had arrived safely. But she's disappeared into America, and I suppose we'll never hear from her again. America is a great whale that swallows Jews whole."

"You're lying to me," my grandmother accused the woman as she studied the suspicious behavior and devious looks of Yetta Soloway, who busied herself silently scouring a burned pot, her way of saying go away I have nothing further to say to you. But other neighbors confirmed the story of Bella's downfall, and my grandmother was determined to save her niece.

Sarah rushed to the local magistrate in the hope of obtaining a court order giving her custody of young Bella so that she could remove her from the brothel. The local magistrate advised her that custody was in the hands of the stepmother, and without the consent of the stepmother, there was little he could do. My grandmother knew that Yetta had probably sold the girl to the Madam of the brothel, and spent whatever money she had made from the transaction.

That very day Sarah went calling at the only brothel in the town. She dressed in her sober black high holy days coat with the indeterminate fur collar and the small garnet pin on the lapel set in pinchbeck gold, a gift from her husband in better days. Sarah carried a large polished rosewood walking stick with an ivory handle inherited from her own mother who had been lame, and she leaned on it in the manner of her invalid mother. Indeed, she seemed possessed by the very spirit of that iron willed lady, a kindness alloyed with unpolished steel, the formula of which was known only to Jewish women of that generation. The women of my family did not believe in a goodness that was not mixed with cunning; my own mother once told me that to be truly good, and she was truly good, one must always use one's wits. Naked, ostentatious goodness without common sense was a vanity, a celebration of self, and a waste of precious feelings. And this was a belief that she had inherited from her own mother, along with a pink cameo pin, a tin chocolate box filled with letters from a Colorado sanitarium, and a pair of soft black leather button up shoes.

Sarah waited for her moment outside the brothel, shaping her strategy. She wanted few if any male customers about when she made her move. It was early afternoon, a slow time at the brothel, when most of the whores were resting, reading, or playing card games; Faro, Vint, or Svoi Koziri; bidding and trumping each other until an early customer might interrupt a good hand. This was the time when Sarah felt she could best rescue the girl. She tugged at the heavy twisted rope that held the cowbell door chimes, and the front door was opened by Anna Bolotnikov herself, a large, stout, amiable woman, a model professional, wearing a striped tailored blouse, a man's satin tie glorified by a dazzling yellow diamond stickpin, her graying hair pulled back into a bun, dressed more like a successful midwife than a Madam. My grandmother asked at once for Bella Busch, her niece.

"There's no one here by that name," Anna replied genially. She turned to the whores and asked. "Do we have a Bella here?" All shook their heads. "We don't have a Bella here," she confirmed. For a moment my grandmother feared that Bella had been sold to yet another brothel, far beyond her limited reach, lost in some sexual wilderness in Siberia. But she was not ready to accept defeat.

"Girls often change their names when they come to work for you, don't they?" my grandmother asked. The Madam nodded her head, agreeing. "Well, perhaps she is here under another name?"

"I would know if that was so," the Madam replied. "I have to register my girls with the prefect of police. They have to show their health certificates. If that Bella of yours was here, I would certainly know."

My grandmother realized that the Madam was telling the truth. It was that evil witch Yetta who had sold the girl to the brothel under an assumed name.

She had faked some papers for her, hoping that Bella would disappear into her false name and her new life.

"I would like to see all your employees," my grandmother said. "You seem a good woman. You can't send me away without the assurance that my niece is not among them. I can't leave and face the ghost of my poor dead brother until you do this."

"You'll go away peacefully if I do this?"

"Yes," my grandmother assured her. "I just want to know that the child is well."

The Madam called into the kitchen. A few of the local Russian girls paraded into the parlor thinking that customers had arrived and that they had been summoned to display themselves. They appeared there with their high broad cheekbones powdered and rouged, their eyebrows plucked into fanciful thin curves, oriental calligraphy strokes that they tweezed with great care, a few with their full breasts exposed to view through a sheer, open blouse. At the end of the line was Cousin Bella looking frightened and frightful in a red wig and an ill-fitting blue silk dress that hung low over her bony shoulders and answering to the name "Svetlana." She smiled wanly at my grandmother who rushed to embrace her. My grandmother, who was not an affectionate woman, allowed

Cousin Bella

the girl to deliver a few wet, teary kisses on her cheek, then held her at arm's length, determined to act calmly, without emotion.

"This is she. This is my Bella," my grandmother announced.

"Ah, if you had only said you were looking for Svetlana," the Madam said.

"I want to take her back home with me," my grandmother said directly. "There has been a terrible mistake."

"I'm afraid that can't be done," the Madam replied. "I have quite a bit of money invested in this girl. She doesn't look it, but she could be a goldmine over time."

"What will it cost me?" My grandmother asked.

"That one is almost priceless," the Madam said. "Don't be deceived by her ugliness, she's very popular with the men. Soldiers love her. That big mouth of hers could suck a regiment dry. Still, I have a heart. I know about family. Five hundred kopeks to buy out her contract."

"I don't have that kind of money!" my grandmother replied. "I'll write a note, and I swear I'll honor the debt, but I want –"

"You want? She wants? They want? I want! I want to own a fancy brothel in Moscow, a palace where aristocrats, hussars, and guardsmen visit," the Madam rejoined impatiently. "I want it filled with Austrian crystal chandeliers and fine porcelain figurines. Look at this shepherdess," she said as she pointed to the small, elegant eighteenth century figurine safely entombed in a glass dome on a spindly Louis fourteenth style table. "It's the finest Meissen," she continued. "Feast your eyes on that sheep she's leading about with the blue bow around its neck; you could shear the wool from the porcelain curls on that one. It took me a year to pay for this. And it's likely I'll never have another like her. I want a dozen more like this one before I die and a porcelain flock of ewes and lambs. Maybe a pretty shepherd boy with a ribbon on his crook to keep her company. I need a little beauty in my life," she insisted, as if all the forces in the world had conspired to keep her from enjoying such beauty.

"These other porcelains are good, but they are nowhere near as fine. You can tell by the delicate fingers, see, they are somewhat webbed, they lack the definition of the other. Some things cannot happen. This girl is here until she works off the five hundred kopecks I paid to her stepmother. She is quite popular with the men, despite her odd, ugly looks. Some men find themselves more easily aroused by plain women rather than the beauties, like Kitty here," she pointed to a pretty short blonde with small Slavic features and bright blue eyes. "These beauties can be too much for them. 'Droopers,' we call 'em. They get the customer aroused, but they are just too lovely for plain country fucking so the poor man begins to droop before he can finish his work. Our Svetlana has a wonderful following. She's a natural. What the eye rejects the cock often delights in."

"I don't need to know all this. I know as much as I need to know. I'm her only blood relation," my grandmother protested. "You must give her over to me."

"Blood relation? What's that? Half the girls here have been sold into the business by blood relations, mothers, fathers, brothers and aunts! This girl has been sold to me with a written contract signed by her guardian. Cash has traded hands. And unless you can repay me with interest, she stays, and you go!"

My grandmother looked around the room and surveyed the six sturdy looking prostitutes who occupied it. She saw the terror and the pleading in Bella's eyes, but she was unable to read the unspoken message. It might have been "Get me out of here, Aunt Sarah." Or more likely, "Go away now and let me live out my wretched life in peace? I can't go back. There is no place left for me in your world!"

A porcelain shepherdess

My grandmother knew only one thing as a certainty. She could not leave her dead brother Abram's child in this place. If she struck the Madam with her stick and attempted to push Bella out the door, she would soon be overpowered and beaten by these sturdy whores, pinned down and tossed out the door, if not put in jail by some magistrate who was a steady customer of the establishment. She was alone, over-matched; even the law was against her. Her decision was sudden, strategic, and powerful. She lifted her cane and brought its ivory handle down with a terrible force on the glass dome that contained the Meissen figurine, shattering the dome. Exploding shards of glass and porcelain flew about the room. No anarchist's bomb, blasting in a crystal palace where a visiting Prince had come to visit, could have caused such devastation. With another stroke she swept the other figurines off the table as she followed through her deadly rampage with an assassin's sure precision, killing the figurines that had landed on the floor with that stout stick as if she was stamping out so many insects.

The Madam looked at her with wonder, rage, and profound despair. Nothing my grandmother might have done could have been this extreme, this terrible to the woman. Anna Bolotnikov knelt down and started to pick up the precious shepherdess, weeping and keening like a mother who had just seen her child run down by a speeding carriage. One of the whores found a tiny arm broken off in the savage attack, another found the crook of the staff, another the head of the sheep, another a shattered shoe, another the beautifully articulated hand with those delicate fingers, but great pieces of the middle section, the beribboned waist and the variegated pink folds of the skirt, seemed to disappear into the ether. They lay on the floor in little patches of powdery porcelain dung beyond any hope of repair. The Madam turned to face my grandmother, about to threaten her with the worst of fates; but my grandmother was too fast for her.

"I am sorry that I destroyed your prized possession," she stated matter-of-factly, "but you failed to listen to me, and you refused to understand that I am a serious woman. Bella is mine. And you have broken her. She is as dear to me as those china tchotchkes were to you. You cannot keep her here. This is just the beginning. If I am forced to leave without her, it will be worse for you later. Someday soon, in the middle of the night, it could be tomorrow, perhaps next month, possibly next year, I will ring this house with kerosene, and ignite it, and you will all die in the flames. Yes, all of you," she said to the astonished women.

"You wouldn't kill Svetlana?" one of the whores queried anxiously. "If you burn this place down she would die with the rest of us."

"As long as this child is here with you she is among the dead," my grandmother said, "so if she dies with you, I save her from a life of humiliation and disease. This is no idle threat," she said to the Madam. "I am prepared to face all the consequences of my act. Are you?"

As Cousin Bella told me so many years later, the Madam took Bella by the shoulders and tossed her roughly into the arms of my grandmother, nearly throwing them both to the ground and ripping the red wig from Bella's head; practical, despite her rage, she figured it could serve another girl later, but letting her depart still wearing the ill-fitting blue gown. "Go! Get out! Go!" she screamed at my grandmother and Bella. They never looked back.

My grandmother and Cousin Bella knew that life after the brothel meant that all doors to a normal life were closed to Bella. There was little chance that she could marry. While whores did marry, and that included Jewish whores, they were women who had put by a great deal of money from their trade, women who found husbands that were none too fastidious about a wife's past – gamblers, deadbeats, peddlers who needed cash to pay debts or start up a business, men with unclean hearts and dirty fingernails. Some of these men enjoyed their wife's degraded condition; it was the best excuse for keeping the woman pressed under the husband's heel or performing circus tricks in the marital bed. Of course, Bella could be sent to America, but once there, despite a change in name, someone would recognize her from the old country, and her secret would be public knowledge in the city ghetto. At my grandmother's house Bella was washed clean, she was sent to the ritual bath, she was never reproached for what had happened to her. All the sin that was, was on the head of Yetta Soloway, my grandmother advised Bella. When Yetta heard of the rescue of Bella, she lay low for a few days, fearing that the Madam would come to her for the return of the kopecks, now long spent, but the Madam appeared to close the book on Bella/Svetlana and did not press charges against my grandmother, that killer of Meissen. She had recognized in Sarah Busch Horowitz a woman whose will was stronger than her own, a woman who would never back down, a force of nature whose family loyalty was an equal in power to sex and hunger, a woman of iron.

Weeks later, when Yetta and her sons were visiting a relative in a suburb of Moscow, they returned to discover that their house had been burned to the ground. A lone brick chimney, charred and desolate, stood among the ashes. Yetta ran at once to the local police and accused my grandmother of the crime, but my grandmother could account for her activities and those of Bella before and during the time when the house burned. She refused to speak further about the accident, for accident it was according to her. "That slob of a Yetta must have left a memorial candle burning when she left her house, with a window open. It doesn't take long for a gust of wind to knock over a candle that would ignite a curtain and set a house afire. It was that, or my dear dead brother's outraged spirit that caused it." But Cousin Bella had her own theory. My grandmother had salted the mind of Anna the Madam with a cabin burning, and the angry Madam, seeking an outlet for her rage at being cheated of money and a prized employee, as well as the destruction of her cherished collection of porcelains, had torched the Soloway's cottage. No one was ever accused, and Yetta Soloway and her sons soon migrated to Chicago, where, Bella was happy to report to me, years later, they were obliged to live out their last miserable days as factory workers who disappeared in a factory fire. Yes, God was just.

*A street in the Jewish
section of Minsk*

II

Bella had been living with my grandmother for a year, working as a seamstress and apprentice-upholsterer in my grandmother's small upholstery business when Max appeared. He had been a draftee, fighting in the Caucuses, and had come home bearing a bullet hole in his shoulder, and a letter of commendation from his commander. "Max Shelupsky, although a Jew, is one of the bravest men I have ever had in my command," the letter started. It went on to commend Max for having single handedly taken on the enemy, stating that his heroism had made possible the escape of several Russian soldiers who had been pinned down by the insurgent artillery fire. But Max found no practical use for the letter. What good was bravery in a world that valued skills? He needed a job and he was determined to immigrate as soon as he had passage money to leave for Hamburg, where he would book passage to America. The new century had begun and he did not want to waste another year of his life in this hopeless, benighted Russia.

When Max entered the upholstery shop, the last person he expected to see was Svetlana, the whore whom he had favored on his trips to the brothel while on leave from the army. He had always asked for her. He found her quiet, soft, and comforting, and if she failed to pretend to the pleasure that other whores had mastered, he did not care. It was a sign of her natural nobility that she did not delight in this desperate animal act, that she indulged a man's desire for fellatio without disgust, nimbly performing her task, taking his organ in her mouth as if it was a flute, and wiping her lips and his penis gently with a towel afterwards. Max appreciated such delicacy. When Max went to embrace Svetlana my grandmother rose and put herself between them. "My dear lady," Max said to my grandmother, "Svetlana and I are old friends from the past."

"If you know her from the past then you don't know her," my grandmother replied. "She is a new person. God and I have given her a new life, and you must not assume that she will now do for free what before she was forced to do as a slave." Bella smiled and nodded. My grandmother's innate respectability was so strong it could sweep a dozen whores under its billowing black skirts and make them emerge in all their lost innocence.

Max claimed that he was seeking a job in the small furniture factory that my grandmother had started in her home. He was a good craftsman, excellent at building frames for any style chair that might be required. "I can do you any kind of Louie," he asserted. "And I'm a master of webbing." In proof he opened up a small valise that contained samples of his carvings, well chiseled roses and leaves, lion's claw feet, excellent dados and beadwork. He hoped that my grandmother would not hold his past knowledge of Svetlana – "Excuse me Madam, Bella," against him. He too had come out of hell, the hell of men dying in meaningless battle, and he wanted a new life. He had killed men, men he did not know, men who might have had wives and children and certainly had immortal souls. Nothing that Bella had done could compare to what he had done in the eye of God. They could both start anew.

It was then that my grandmother offered him Bella's hand in marriage in exchange for employment. She would call his bluff, all that past is past stuff; it was "marry her or leave now."

"I'd be honored," Max asserted.

"You'd better be," my grandmother stated, "because there is no finer woman than my niece Bella."

A wedding was hastily arranged. The marriage was recorded, but there was no honeymoon, not even a schnapps and shnecken party celebrating the union. Bella and Max worked in the upholstery shop for a year, saving for their passage to America. They booked passage with my grandmother whose sister-in-law Maryasha had finally sent the passage money for her and the four children. There was urgency to my grandmother's decision. She was nearly thirty-five, and felt that she had not long to live. Blood had already appeared like a red carnation on her cotton handkerchiefs, and she knew what that meant. And if Bella's experience had taught her anything, she knew it was dangerous to leave her young children in the hands of strangers, particularly her youngest, my mother Libby, who at two years old, was showing signs of an astonishing beauty, a terrifying beauty, a perfection which God might punish, for it rarely appeared in this life; skin, eyes, teeth, hair, nose, chin, all of it better than any porcelain fashion doll crafted in Germany by the finest of artisans. Such beauty challenged the world, and it could only be destroyed in a place like Russia. She had to get the child to safety in America.

We'll get to my mother, Libby of the astonishing beauty, and my grandparents at another time, but for now, let us stay with the Max and Bella Shelupsky marriage, one that would see a golden anniversary and an extraordinary event in between.

Arriving in America, Max landed a job as a salesman in a furniture showroom on Essex Street which offered one free upholstered side chair and footstool with every sofa ordered, and the promise of interest free time payments, then new to business on the lower East Side. Bella continued to make slipcovers. America was the perfect venue for her slipcovers at that time. It was a world that considered it wasteful, almost shameful, to show a naked sofa or chair, and furniture once purchased was meant to last a lifetime, thus the need for slipcovers. Everything had to be covered, and the bright paisley cotton prints were favored for concealing the delicate silk brocade upholstery. The Shelupskys did not starve, but they did not prosper, they were never to leave the Lower East Side, and they lived out their long lives on Rivington Street. Food was always on the table, obligations were always met, and the past was well behind them. If anyone could recognize Bella Shelupsky as Svetlana the whore of Anna Bolotnikov's Minsk brothel, they never dared to show it, for Max was a large, strong man, and my grandmother, Bella's guardian, was someone you did not wish to offend. It was rumored that she had the evil eye; that a scowl from her could bring down ruin upon you. My mother always felt that it was her mother, Sarah herself, who sent this story of her demonic look out into the world,

The Lower East Side in 1903

using it as a source of power in that unruly neighborhood. It helped to conceal my grandmother's absolute kindness, which would have made her appear weak and vulnerable in that crowded, grasping, coughing world.

Cousin Bella guarded her own secret, not so much for herself, but for her beloved Max. The world was not kind enough to understand his goodness and would regard his tender love for her as stupidity, simple mindedness. They would say that he had been hoodwinked, and he would be mocked. But they would never know. Her secret was protected by her ugliness. Women who looked like this had an inborn respectability that could never be doubted. The marriage was a happy one, Max and Bella delighted in each other. He was a man of few words and she was a woman of many, none of them comprehensible to the English speaking world. He had mastered enough English to work in the store, and she had attended night school to learn the new language but she mainly spoke Yiddish or Russian as the mood or circumstance took her, mixing them into a personal patois that was good enough for shopping, and making slipcovers.

If there was any shadow over the marriage it was Bella's failure to have children. They tried, she told me, but it was not meant to be. She went to the local synagogue and prayed for a child, she consulted a rabbi, a doctor and a midwife, she even ventured uptown to St. Patrick's Cathedral and lit a candle before an image of the virgin – she was not one to refuse help from anyone with a reputation for answering prayers, but she never became pregnant. She wondered if something had happened to her womb in that brothel that had kept her from conceiving a child, but there was little she could do about her maternal longing until the arrival of Baby Rivka.

III

The Shelupskys supplemented their meager income by renting out a spare room to transient immigrants. One day, a dark, pretty young woman who introduced herself as Mrs. Goldie Shapiro took the room for one month for herself and her infant daughter Rivka. Goldie Shapiro told the Shelupskys that she was "a desperate seeker." She had come from Poland in search of a husband who had come to America a year before, leaving her to face the birth of her daughter, Rivka, alone in Europe. At first there were letters from various addresses on the lower East Side, and then none. Finally, a letter arrived from a female relative in San Francisco claiming that she had seen Sol Shapiro, the errant husband, moving a pushcart along Grand Avenue, selling embroidered satin ribbons and silk frog fastenings to Chinese women. It was Goldie's hope that she could find the sweet but feckless Sol in San Francisco, but the expense and the logistics of booking passage from Poland to the West Coast of America with a baby in

Immigrants at Ellis Island

her arms had been too much for her. Better that first she came east and worked till she could pay for train fare to San Francisco. And so she found employment running a knitting machine in a sweater factory, leaving the baby Rivka in the care of Cousin Bella, at first with the promise of a fee, but in time Bella found herself an unpaid caretaker of the delightful infant.

Bella came to love the child fiercely, and dreaded the day when Goldie Shapiro would depart for San Francisco with the baby on her desperate husband hunt. Goldie had been obliged to work for six months to save enough for the train fare and a month's living in San Francisco. When Goldie came to say goodbye, Bella faced the woman stoically; this was the punishment she deserved. She knew she had done a wicked thing. During Goldie's long working hours she had not discouraged the infant Rivka from calling her Momma, she had pointed to herself and mouthed the word, and then she had answered to the name and kissed the fingers of the infant. Indeed, the child had seen more of Bella than of Goldie. Bella feared that God had punished her for her wickedness, for what could be as dreadful as coveting and stealing the love of another woman's child?

To Bella's astonishment, Goldie pleaded for more help. "I know it's a terrible thing to ask of you, but I must ask, for the baby's sake and for mine. If I take the child with me to San Francisco, she might become ill on the long journey, I would have no place to keep her as I searched San Francisco for her father, Sol Shapiro. I might never find him there, and the burden of a small child would weigh so heavily upon me that it would surely sink me. Can you? Would you keep Rivka here for me? When I come back for her, I will pay you for your care. And I will come back within a few months, no matter what happens. I will write to you weekly about my progress, and you will write to me telling me about the baby. If I am not able to reward you properly in this life for your goodness, surely God will reward you in the next," she assured Cousin Bella. Bella agreed at once, and thanked God for this chance to spend more time with the beloved child.

Goldie departed leaving Bella with the child. My grandmother warned Bella against the arrangement. "What if she doesn't come back for years, and you form an attachment to the child? There's only heartbreak in this for you when she comes to claim her."

"So?" Bella replied. "Haven't I known heartbreak before? And haven't I survived it? I will be careful, Aunt Sarah, I promise you."

Max had also warned his wife against growing too fond of the infant. "She will come back for her, and it will leave you too sad and broken to mend your life again. God only gives us one chance at a new life," he told her, and she knew what he meant. Bella, usually compliant, called him a fool, and assured him that if the child were taken from her tomorrow, she would go on with her life, thankful that she had had her even for this short time. "I have survived worse than you could ever know," she said.

Every day that passed she faced a fear of what might arrive in the mail. But Goldie Shapiro, after sending a few postcards from San Francisco, ugly tintypes of tramcars careening down steep hills, stopped writing altogether. On the day when Rivka was one year old, Bella renamed her Pauline, after *The Perils of Pauline*, which she had seen in a nickelodeon. Max suspected that Bella was trying to hide the girl under a new name, but there was nothing to be done about it. He could not continue to call the child Rivka when Bella was calling her Pauline. At six Pauline was as beautiful a child as had been entered into the Rivington Street Grammar School. She had a gift for drawing and a talent for languages, already fluent in Russian, Polish, German, and Yiddish. She knew so much for a small, pretty child, but there was one fact she did not know, and would not for years to come. She did not know that Bella was not her mother, and that Max was not her father. Max had wanted to tell her, but Bella has threatened to leave him if he did.

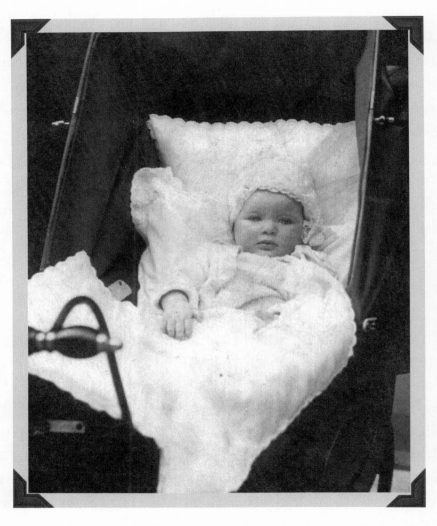

Baby Rivka (Pauline)

"And how would you live if you did?" he asked. "I can do more than make slipcovers," Bella replied running her index finger through a circle she made with her thumb and pinky on her other hand, thereby ending the argument.

Max had even consulted with a lawyer about the possibility of adopting Pauline, but he had been told that there was no way to adopt the child on grounds of abandonment before the requisite seven years. And if they started such proceedings there was no saying that the Surrogate Court might not take the child from their home and place her in an institution, after all, they were not blood relatives. The natural parents might return at any time, claim the child, and have every legal right to do so.

Six days before Pauline's seventh birthday, a letter arrived from San Francisco. It was the dreaded letter from Goldie Shapiro. "My dear Bella, how do I start? Where do I start? When I left for San Francisco I had promised, indeed I had meant to write you weekly. But I fell ill upon arriving in this city, and what strength I had was spent on the search for my Sol Shapiro. You would think that with the very small Jewish community they have here in this land of rough goyem Sol would be easy to find. But he had never attended any of the synagogues, nor was he living in the small community off Market Street where the other Polish Jews had settled. I walked the streets searching for him, but I never found him or anyone who had seen him. I am afraid that the failure of my mission undid me. I got a job as a factory worker making leather handbags, and I settled down to a solitary existence. How could I come back and reclaim my beloved Rivka? Who would look after her here, where I had no friends or family? Before I knew it a few years had passed, and I had not written to you. Then one day I decided to visit the great world's fair here. And it was at that fair that I came upon Sol, who stood outside the lovely ornamental metal gates with his pushcart. You cannot imagine the kisses, the tears, and the embraces. He claimed that he had tried to find me and failed, but he had never given up hope that someday we would be together again. I told him of my hunt for him and of our child Rivka who was living with a distant relative in New York. Forgive me for that, but I could not tell him that I had left our child with a stranger. And you were kinder to me than any relative of mine, so how could you be a stranger? He said he longed to see the child, but there was no way we could afford to reclaim her at this time. If she was well cared for, we could do that later. For now we would start our new life in the west. Within a year we had a son, Grover Cleveland Shapiro, and life became very good for us. Sol had started a small dry goods store with his savings, and we prospered. And now, at long last, we are ready to reclaim our own dear Rivka. The three hundred dollars that I send you enclosed should help cover the costs you have had for maintaining my dear child. If it's more, let me know. Can you send me a photograph of her? I would like to know what she looks like before I come for her next month. Yes, I am planning to travel east for her soon. God bless you for your kindness to a lost woman and her child. Goldie Shapiro."

Bella did not consider showing the letter to Max. She knew he would have only one reply. "We must give up the child." That was not an answer to her; it was a death sentence. She knew she could not outlive the loss of Pauline. How convenient of this awful Goldie and the slippery Sol to leave the child in her care, so that they could work their shop and prosper. They had shown her no mercy in letting her raise and love this wonderful child. Why should she give them better than what she got? They did not love this child. She was lost property, a misplaced hat or glove, not a person to them, and they came for her as proprietors, claimants, not as parents. She did not consult my grandmother, who would certainly agree with

Rivka Shapiro

October 7, 1901 - February 2, 1903

חָקָל הָוֹהְיַו ,וֹתָנ הָוֹהְי

Rivka's gravestone as described by Bella

Max, and together form a wall of opposition to her plan. No, she went ahead and wrote the letter.

"My dear Goldie, I was happy to hear from you at long last, I had given you up for dead, but I must reply to your letter with a heavy heart. Five years ago our darling Rivka took ill with the diphtheria and died. I will not send a picture of her, who needs such grief? But I am enclosing one of her headstone in the Jewish Workers Circle cemetery where she rests in peace. I am keeping your money, which will cover what I was forced to spend for the gravestone and burial costs. With great sadness and condolences from your friend, Bella Shelupsky."

Bella knew that the letter alone might not do the work for her, so she rushed to a stonecutter, and offering him double his fees, had a small headstone carved within a few hours. It had Rivka's name, date of birth and death chiseled in it with a short Hebrew prayer beneath ("The Lord giveth and the Lord hath taken away"). For five dollars more she bought a beautiful funeral wreath. For another ten dollars the stonecutter took her in his horse drawn delivery cart to Central Park where she placed the small gravestone upright, supported by some unseen rocks, laid the wreath at its foot, and using Max's Brownie camera, took a roll of film of the gravesite. She did not send it to Kodak for development, but for ten dollars more she found a professional portrait photographer on Allen Street who would develop the film that very afternoon. Within twenty-four hours, the letter, with the photograph of the gravesite, was mailed to San Francisco. A mournful letter came back from Goldie, thanking Bella for her care of the late, unfortunate child, the darling, short-lived Rivka. She insisted that Bella keep the money nevertheless and said that she would communicate with her no further. It must almost be as painful to Bella, who had raised this child like a mother, as it was to Goldie, the grieving mother who would never have the joy of raising that child.

IV

And so twenty years passed without any stranger discovering Bella's guilty secret. My grandmother decided that Bella's life had been hard enough, and this was God's way of rewarding her for her complete reformation. Pauline was now twenty-two – a graduate of the Verna Moon secretarial school – and working as a secretary bookkeeper at a very important lawyer's office. Bella claimed that it was that of Samuel Liebowitz, criminal lawyer, and later famous for his defense of the Scottsboro Boys, but when I checked it seemed that a young Liebowitz would have just been starting out on his own career, and that it was some other law firm. It was clear that she wanted to give Pauline's job the greatest importance to show that the girl had thrived under her care. Pauline had indeed grown into a tall, easygoing, cheerful young woman. Some commented that there was no resemblance between her and the iron haired, plain faced Bella, but they noted a resemblance to Max, who still displayed his good looking regular features in his work worn face.

Despite the fact that she was now earning a good living, Pauline had not left the family apartment on Rivington Street to strike out on her own. She had complained about the toilet in the hallway that was always stuffed, and the primitive kitchen, but she loved her parents and knew that leaving them before marriage was out of the question. When she weighed their worrying about her against her own independence, their worry always won out.

It was while Pauline was at work uptown, and Bella was at home putting the trim on a set of love-seat slipcovers, that twenty-one-year-old Grover Cleveland Shapiro knocked at Cousin Bella's door. He was a good-looking, gentle, well-spoken man whose voice was that of the new America, a voice without accent, without foreign roots. He had the deep green eyes, thick blonde hair and the perfect teeth of a movie star. Bella knew at once who he was and where he had come from. He asked if she remembered his late mother, Goldie Shapiro, while his mother was living on the lower East Side. After his mother's death he had discovered an envelope addressed to his mother with the return address of a Bella Shelupsky on Rivington Street. If she had written to his mother, surely she must have known her? Bella had dreaded this day, but she was prepared for it. She answered him in her

Russo-Yiddish patois, and to her amazement he understood it. He told her that he had spent his early years among immigrants.

"I had so many boarders here, it is hard to tell one from another," Cousin Bella replied. "Shapiro? Goldie? There was a Goldie...no...it was a Gertrude Fuchs who lived here one summer for a few days, perhaps a week. But no Goldie that I can recall. No, not familiar." He produced the envelope and removed from it a photograph of his mother, taken a few years after she had arrived in San Francisco. "No," Bella replied. "Such a lovely face I would remember. As far as the envelope, I was probably sending her some mail. We had so many boarders those days, some stayed a week, some a few days, she was probably an overnighter – a one night boarder – but if I got a letter for any one of them, I always sent it on, even though I had to pay for the postage. A letter is a sacred trust. Still, I can't be expected to remember all of them. Why are you looking for people who knew her?"

As he sipped his glass of tea, he explained that his mother had died thirteen years before, and his father had died shortly thereafter. He was all of seven years old when he was placed in the St. Francis Catholic Boys Orphanage. There was no Jewish orphanage in San Francisco at that time, nor could the

The St. Francis Orphan Asylum,
Watsonville, California

city guardians find any living relatives in California so he was given over to the only institution that would take him. He stayed in the orphanage until he was sixteen, when he was released in his own charge, with a letter recommending him as a boy of impeccable character and good habits. Although he had been baptized and had served as an altar boy, he never forgot his Jewish family and his Jewish roots. He had worked hard, first as a stock-boy and later as a clerk at Gumps Department Store, but he found life as a salesman dull and restrictive. Two years at San Francisco School of Industrial Technology had given him a degree as a draughtsman in engineering and architectural rendering, and he had then worked as an assistant to an engineer, drawing bridges and public monuments in the Bay area. He had been happy in that work, but he had felt discontented, lonely, a shy man without real friends and family. His good looks had made people expect a racy confidence, when all he had to offer the world was a respectful reticence. It was then he had decided to come east and try to track down his mother's friends, people who might have known her while she was living on Rivington Street. He wanted to find his past to ease his burden of loneliness. He knew it was Rivington Street, because she had mentioned it to him once, and then there was the envelope addressed to his mother, with Bella's name and address on the back flap. He was an only child; there had been a sister he had never known; his mother spoke of her dying young. It was hard to have no one to share one's pain and one's joy, but he needed some fuller memories, some history to connect him to the world.

Later, Bella conceded that if she had only spoken up then, she might have averted all that was to follow. But the truth no longer existed for her as a possibility. There was no Rivka. Rivka was dead. Pauline was her daughter, she was God's gift to her, compensation for her cruel life in that brothel, and she would not renounce this gift in order to satisfy the emotional hunger of this strange, lost boy and resurrect the long dead Rivka so that he might have a living sister. Oh, but she was right to keep Pauline innocent of her past, she told herself, and to do all that she had done. Those foolish parents of Pauline's did not even have the decency to stay alive for their son. Why the poor girl might have been placed like her brother in a Catholic orphanage, or worse, like herself, found herself in the hands of a whorehouse Madam. Bella told him that his was an impossible quest; he might as well go back to Belarus, Russia or Poland or wherever his mother had come from in order to find a lost family. This was

America. Here people broke their natural ties with the family in the pursuit of survival, which soon enough became success, or abject failure. Bella offered to hold on to the photograph of the dead Goldie and show it around the neighborhood for him in case someone – if that would help. Grover Cleveland Shapiro thanked Cousin Bella for her offer but decided he would bring his mother's photograph with him as he canvassed the neighborhood for someone who might remember her. Bella took comfort in this, for there were few of the original Rivington Street settlers about.

One of the hazards of
living in Flatbush

V

In the past few years there had been a great migration from Rivington Street. Almost alone among those old timers, Bella and Max had stayed on, finding no lure in the Flatbush of Brooklyn or the Tremont Avenue of the Bronx. Subways, elevated tracks, might carry you back and forth into the city where you worked, reading *The Daily Mirror* on cane cushioned seats, and take you back home to a new apartment with a private bathroom and strip of hedges but who needed a strip of hedges? You want trees? Go back to Russia, where the forests were thick and verdant. Who needed nature? Nature was for the goyim. Nature was for fools. She found safety and comfort in these familiar, narrow soiled streets, and she would never leave them.

Pauline had flourished here. That girl did not need to join the snobbish young beauties of the Bronx and meet some hoity-toity friend to unsettle her girl's homespun views. Here, Bella knew all the dangers that might face her child; a sly shopkeeper who might offer a young girl a new dress in exchange for helping her put it on, a stray cat who might spring out of a garbage can to attack you when startled. Men would be pushing their bodies against a young girl's in the crowded streets and subways. But who knew what dangers awaited those who made the reckless relocation to the outer boroughs? In Brooklyn elevated trains could derail and topple over onto the streets killing their passengers and innocent pedestrians below. Bella had seen the pictures. Murdered bodies were discovered daily on the empty lots of the Bronx and Brooklyn, behind signs that promised the building of a new movie theatre on this site. Chaos reigned in the sparsely settled outer boroughs while order could be found in the chaos of the crowds on Rivington Street.

Time had proven her right. Pauline had grown up strong, beautiful and safe, and she would someday meet a young lawyer at the Liebowitz office who would love her at once, shyly court her, and end by producing an engagement ring, a wedding at the East Side community house, and in time a good family. How could it be otherwise? They would marry, have two children, and her life would run according to the arcane, hidden rules of happiness, which Bella had never mastered, but which existed for beautiful people like Pauline and her someday husband, all played out in a house in Jersey, with chocolate covered children's parties and sleek motor cars. But until then, Pauline was safe – satisfied that she was the only child of Max and Bella Shelupsky. The only question about her past had to do with her place of birth. "Don't tell me I was born in Russia or Poland?" she once queried, fearful that she could be thought of as a greenhorn. Because it came from Pauline, certain questions were commands.

"No," Bella replied, firmly. "You are one hundred percent American, born here one year after your father and I had settled into Rivington Street.

When my grandmother died, during the First World War of the consumption that she had battled for years, Bella felt both grief and relief. The last, the only witness to the past, aside from Max, was now in her grave. The secret of Pauline's birth had died with Bella's savior.

Bella had been very careful. A birth certificate had been forged for a home birth for a Pauline Shelupsky years ago, shortly after she purchased the gravestone and sent the picture out west. Pauline's certificate of excellence from the secretarial school was all she needed to get her safely through this life; other papers would be "lost" or "stolen." Bella had read a serialized version of *Stella Dallas*, by Olive Higgins Proudie, in a Yiddish translation. It was her personal guide. Should she ever find herself standing in the

Samuel Goldwyn presents

The Henry King Production

"Stella Dallas"

Olive Higgins Proudie's novel would
first reach the screen in 1925

way of a grand marriage for Pauline, she would leave her for life, as the love besotted Stella did for her daughter, Lollie. But in her heart she knew that was for goyim, and it seemed unlikely that any Jewish family would turn up their noses at her beautiful, well-mannered Pauline simply because Max and Bella were working class folks from the Lower East Side. No, her very background was proof of how superior Pauline was, because she had risen above it so easily. Other girls might be as pretty or as smart, but Bella knew that Pauline had mastered the trick of America. She had charm, and charm was currency in the new world.

It was one of those rare days when Bella was out of the flat, cutting a slipcover in the Bronx, that Grover Cleveland Shapiro knocked on the Shelupsky door again. Alone among all the dozens he had queried, there was a peddler named Ben Berkowitz who had recalled his mother's face from the photograph and told him that the woman was most definitely a boarder with the Shelupskys for a few months at the turn of the century. Grover returned to the Shelupsky flat late that afternoon to press Bella to remember more about the woman in the picture, but once he saw Pauline, the interest in his parentage seemed secondary to his admiration for this beautiful young woman.

Pauline studied the photograph and said that she knew nothing of his mother. But she understood his quest. The sweet certainty of her own parentage, the love that Bella and Max had invariably shown her, this was the rock on which she had built her life. It was terrible to imagine a child like Grover Cleveland Shapiro growing up amongst strangers in a Catholic orphanage where there were only rules and gruesome crosses with bleeding Christs wearing crowns of thorns, and no love. She looked at him and saw not only the best looking young man she had ever seen, but also a man who needed help. The nature of that help was difficult to determine, but it didn't matter, she would provide it.

Bella returned to Rivington Street to find the young man and Pauline going over the photographic scrapbook that Max had kept of Pauline's childhood. The young man held the large green leather book in his hands, and was jesting about some snapshot of the three year old Pauline, in which she sobbed for the camera as her cotton diaper fell around her feet. Bella went over to him and slammed the book shut hard on his fingers.

"What are you doing back here?" she demanded. "I have nothing more to say to you. I told you that I did not know your mother. Who knows if such a woman ever existed? Perhaps you are some kind of criminal trickster who gets into people's homes with this cock and bull story of a missing mother. You like going to strangers' doors? Go sell encyclopedias!" she commanded with a brutality that Pauline had never heard before.

Now she turned her wrath on Pauline, and the girl was amazed by it. "I thought I raised you better than to invite young men into our home without a chaperone. Who knows what he is? Certainly a stranger. Possibly a thief? A rapist? An assassin? And you open the door for this one? Nice, respectable Fuller Brush men are not allowed inside this apartment, and this nobody from nowhere comes here and you let him in? Pauline, I thought you were smarter than that. You shame me with this... this stupidity!"

To her own surprise, Pauline began to cry, and the young man stepped forward to apologize for the intrusion. He explained that he had come back only after speaking with the peddler who claimed that his mother *had* lived as a roomer in the Shelupsky apartment some twenty years before. Would Bella just concentrate and think harder about this woman, as he held out the photograph again?

"Now, I remember her," Bella said bitterly. "She came with references from the Tsarina of Russia! She claimed to be the Crown Princess Anastasia, so you my boy, must be the heir to the throne of Russia. Keep looking for her Alexei Nikolayevich. Not only will you find a mother but you'll find a throne!"

What shocked Pauline was not merely the savage, mocking tone, but the anger that broke through it. It was not mere dislike for a young man who had violated her mother's sense of protocol, but a palpable hatred for him, like a wary animal faced by one who threatened the very core of her existence.

"Get out!" Bella ordered. "Don't come back here. If you do I will call upon some friends to see to it that you do not bother me and my family again." This was no idle threat. Bella had maintained good relations with members of the Jewish gangs who now controlled the laundry business in the city. "Little Jeff Heinz" – later to become my Uncle Mike – who was courting my mother's older sister, Ida Horowitz, was one who would think nothing of smashing this man's skull in, if Bella had asked him to do so. She had been kind to Little Jeff in his childhood, and was known to all the street gangs as one of the good women who kept the community going with noodle pudding, beef-flanken, and a supply of surgical bandages that were at the ready for bruised heads and knees. These men had been charged with the protection of Pauline as a child, making it possible for Bella to work away from home and never worry about Pauline's safety. Pauline knew this, but she had never heard her mother raise her voice in a threat. She turned to Grover Cleveland Shapiro, and told him that it was better that he go. He mumbled an apology to Bella and left the apartment. Pauline stared at her mother in anger and disbelief.

"How could you be so cruel, Mama? So rude?" Pauline demanded.

"I could. I did. I can," Bella replied. "This was nothing to what will happen to him should he be stupid enough to return here."

Pauline and Grover would never again meet on Rivington Street. The platforms of the elevated trains along Third Avenue, the city parks, and a coffee shop in Times Square where they could get lost in the crowds would serve as the safe places for their rendezvous. They were always changing the place of their meetings, but never leaving each other until another meeting had been arranged. By this time he had her office telephone number, and he called so often that the switchboard operator began to tease Pauline about her secret admirer. Within a month hands had been held, kisses had been exchanged, vows made, and Pauline assured him that Bella and Max would come around and accept him as soon as they saw him as a steady worker and a serious suitor. Bella had somehow mistaken him for a drifter, it was only a matter of Grover Cleveland finding the right

New York's Times Square in the 1920s

job, and letting time settle the matter. Bella remained vigilant, but for all her snooping in Pauline's bureau drawers and pillowcases and flipping pages of the encyclopedia in Pauline's room for hidden missives, she discovered no sign of these meetings. Pauline seemed cheerful, obedient, the old Pauline. The only noticeable change was that Sam Bronstein, one of her beaus, stopped taking her to the movies on the weekend and Pauline claimed to have lost interest in this prosperous owner of a cigar shop on 54th Street. Other boyfriends were discouraged. Max worried that Pauline was shutting herself off from others of her age, but Bella assured him that when the right man appeared, they would know it. And so would Pauline. Bella was so grateful that Grover Cleveland Shapiro had disappeared from their life, that she would now settle for far less in the way of a mate for the beloved child. Looks would no longer matter. "God, you can forget the tall, handsome rich man I prayed for. I was a stupid, greedy woman then. A good heart coupled with a steady small business is all that I ask for her now." It was important that a match be made and a marriage arranged as soon as possible.

One day, Bella recklessly asked Pauline if she had run into that crazy Grover Cleveland boy, and Pauline shook her head and answered, "No! Do you think he would come back here after the way you treated him?" It was the first lie that Pauline had ever told her mother, but she felt no guilt. Her mother was ignorant, she had the immigrant's fear of strangers; it was a greenhorn's failing, and although she loved her mother none the less, she felt no need to respect her mother's old world superstitions.

Grover Cleveland Shapiro found work as an architectural draughtsman. The architects were impressed by his sure, clear renderings, his freehand ability to draw the straightest of lines and the roundest of circles, his ability to give dimension to ornamentation, and his hard working ethic. His boss had called him "My young Prince of the pencil." Architecture was not then a trade that was open to Jews, but they felt that no client would suspect that this fair-haired boy from the west was Jewish, so they took to calling him "Mr. Sharp" and he was thus gainfully employed. He told his bosses that he had to make a certain sum, because he planned to marry shortly, and they settled on a salary that was higher than Grover Cleveland had ever earned before, but still less than he needed to take on a wife.

"Don't worry about money," Pauline assured her lover. "I can keep working until we have a baby, and by that time, you should be advanced in your career."

She assured him that she was going to inform her folks of their plans very soon. "You have a good job now," she continued. "How could they object?"

"You know I've never had a bar mitzvah," Grover Cleveland admitted.

"You're man enough for me," Pauline replied seductively.

It was now that Grover Cleveland presented her with a small diamond ring that he had purchased for two hundred dollars from "Jake the Jeweler," whose guarantee of "I'll buy it back for twice what you paid if you find it cheaper elsewhere" came with every purchase.

"He'll take it back if you don't like it," her lover told Pauline.

"I love it," Pauline replied. This was the culmination of all her romantic fancies – only instead of watching lovers spooning in a movie or looking at models of lovers posing in an advertisement for chocolates, it was she, Pauline and her Grover who were now the leading figures in their own love story. It might lack a silver moon and some golden stars but it was all the more wonderfully real for that.

It was on the following Sunday that Pauline decided to present the fait accompli of the engagement to her parents. She had covered her hand with a

A romantic postcard from the 1920s

dishcloth as she helped with the serving, but as she sat down she held up her finger and offered it to them to admire.

"When? Who?" Bella asked.

"When? This week. Who? Grover Cleveland Shapiro. The young man who came around looking for his mother. We have been seeing each other. I know Momma you didn't like him but he has a wonderful job now, and we love each other. And once you get to know him as I do you –"

"You cannot!" Bella shouted.

"Why not? Because you took some crazy dislike for him?"

"Trust me. There are reasons that go beyond liking or disliking. He could be the best man in the world, and you still could not marry him."

"Why is that?" Pauline asked defiantly, ready to tear down any new objection offered. She suspected it was the Catholic upbringing, the lack of a Jewish identity that his years in San Francisco had denied him; that this was the source of Bella's objections. "You think he's too young for me? So he's only twenty. But he's an old twenty. You think he's a goy and I'm marrying out of the faith? Well, he's as Jewish as any man on Rivington Street. Why, he had a bris and –"

"How would you know that?" Bella asked.

"Trust me, I do," Pauline replied, unwilling to deny any part of the intimacy that had developed between her and Grover Cleveland; the meetings in his rooming house on Saturday afternoons which had led to the mutual loss of their virginities.

"Then this is worse than I feared," Bella said, turning to Max. She kept silent for a moment, pondering the way she might announce the fact and cause the least injury to her beloved daughter. She knew there was no good way, and only one way, so she took it.

"This Grover Cleveland Shapiro is your brother."

"Are you saying that he is your son?" Pauline asked, fearful that her mother had gone mad without any warning signs other than the crazy look in her eyes.

"No!" Bella replied. Then she told her about Goldie Shapiro, and what she, Bella, had done to conceal the facts of Pauline's birth from Pauline. It had been a sin, perhaps a crime, but Pauline could understand the depths of her love for her, and look what Pauline had been spared by that deception. If she had returned the child to her rightful mother, Pauline would have had to spend her youth in some Catholic orphanage under the harsh discipline of nuns who beat her with whips, mocked her name of Rivka, or worse, converted her to their faith. As Pauline, the daughter of Max and Bella Shelupsky, she had known nothing but care and love, and surely God had guided Bella's hand in this by removing her from the very Rivka-ness that would have been her downfall.

"I don't believe you," Pauline stated. "You'd do anything to keep us from marrying. Momma, I'm sorry that this gives you such grief, but my entire happiness depends upon my marrying Grover Cleveland Shapiro."

"Max, tell her!" Bella commanded.

"It's the truth," Max said softly. "Marry this man and you commit a crime against God's law and man's. Nature will not suffer this."

"You'd say anything to back her up. If he had an older sister, don't you think he would know about that? His mother would have said something about her."

"Not if the woman believed that the child had died. I even had a gravestone carved with your birth name on it and sent her a picture. Oh, Pauline, we loved you so much; there was nothing we wouldn't do."

"Did you know about this gravestone?" Pauline asked Max.

"No," he replied. "But there was nothing your mother wouldn't have done to protect you."

"My mother? Which one is it? Bella Shelupsky or Goldie Shapiro? I don't know why you two are doing this. It's wicked, Momma, wicked, but I'm not fooled by you."

Pauline returned to Grover Cleveland's room and told him that her parents were so far gone into madness there was no chance that they would approve of their marriage. The following day they went to the city hall and were married by a clerk of the Civil Court. Pauline wore a rose colored woolen suit and a rose straw hat purchased at Macy's Little Shop, and Grover Cleveland was handsome in his new dark blue serge suit – "the Bar Mitzvah suit I never had," he jested. And so they became Mr. and Mrs. Grover Cleveland Sharp. Grover Cleveland had juggled the letters in Shapiro to advance with greater ease in his world of architecture.

VI

It has never been very clear as to how the story became public. Pauline was pregnant. Bella had gone into a deep mourning when a local Rabbi who held services in a small, converted dry goods store two houses down from the Shelupskys visited her. Max had worried about the health of his wife who had taken to her bed, ate next to nothing, maybe half a bagel and some weak tea, and would speak with nobody about her troubles. As a last resort he sent for the Rabbi to counsel the grieving woman. The Rabbi came, he heard the story, and told Bella that she must report this to the civil authorities. Bella refused to do so. A troubled Rabbi reported the news to his new wife, whose eldest son a newspaper reporter, checked the public records at Ellis Island and found the document that showed that a Goldie Shapiro had immigrated to America in 1902, together with a six months old child, a daughter. Then he phoned the San Francisco hall of records and discovered a registered birth in 1904 of Grover Cleveland Shapiro to this same Goldie Shapiro.

Bella and Max at Coney Island

The reporter tracked the newlyweds to their fourth floor room in the West Eighties. When he knocked on the door, his cameraman took the flash photo of the startled Pauline and the outraged Grover Cleveland. The couple refused an interview with the paper, although Pauline was heard to say that her mother Bella Shelupsky had so disapproved of their marriage that she had concocted a libelous fiction about the backgrounds of the bride and groom. The photographer lightened Pauline's hair on the negative and curled it slightly, retouching the doctored pictures so that in every case the resemblance between Pauline and the fair haired Grover Cleveland was unmistakably that of brother and sister. The story took on another dimension when the reporter discovered that Pauline had visited a settlement house where she had been given prenatal advice. "What kind of monster will spring from this tragedy?" the paper queried in a headline of eighteen point type, inviting its readers to comment on the story in the "What would you do if it happened to you?" column.

Never in the history of that paper had its readers sent in so much mail. At least half the correspondents blamed the tragedy on the lies of Bella Shelupsky, a woman who had tricked a poor, lost woman out of her child. Others pointed to the degraded morals of immigrant women who dropped their newborns like so many unwanted kittens on a stranger's doorstep. Soon, all the local and national papers got wind of the story. The moralists and reformers amongst them – and there were many – wrote that this could not have happened if sanitary conditions in the ghetto had been improved, something they had been demanding for years. How could society expect morals from people who live in such filth and squalor? A photograph of the overstuffed toilet in the Shelupsky tenement's hallway appeared beside a beautiful High School graduation portrait of Pauline whose innocent smile appeared wantonly knowing in the context of the story.

Grover Cleveland's architectural firm was careful not to fire Grover Cleveland, an act that might bring the wrong kind of attention to them with its notoriety. They offered him a leave of absence to straighten out his affairs and advised him that he would only be welcomed back once he had taken the proper step of an annulment. They even offered him the legal advice of their staff attorney, who put in motion a petition of annulment, based upon deception. Pauline and Grover Cleveland Sharp obtained their annulment. The child was born normal in all ways, a reproof to the doctors and the moralists who predicted multiple heads, clubfeet, fourteen fingers, and a spectacular hair-lip. Shortly after his birth Pauline advised the Shelupskys that she could not, would not, raise such a child. Without a moment's hesitation Cousin Bella took the baby as her own, and Seymour Shelupsky as he was later called, grew into a bright, lively child, devoted to the self-proclaimed grandparents who raised him. Pauline moved to Chicago, and Grover Cleveland left for the far west, never to be heard from again. The following fall, just when Bella thought that the story had quieted down and disappeared, a popular new tragedy appeared on the Yiddish stage on Second Avenue, or so she advised me on that fateful day when she told me her story. Bella claimed that it was entitled *My Brother, My Love*. She said with some pride that the patrons were warned to come armed with several handkerchiefs; nobody could leave this theatre with a dry eye. But the run was short when, according to Bella, the star fell into the orchestra pit in a fit of breast beating, dislocating his thighbone, and his leading actress left the stage accusing him of ruining her best scene by his clumsy, hammy dive into the orchestra pit.

Bella further claimed that F.W. Murnau, the famed pioneer film director in Berlin, heard the story of the incestuous lovers and prepared a treatment of it

Lil Dagover

for the silent screen, transporting the events to Bavaria and trading on the Wagnerian parallels by calling the two lovers Siegfried and Sieglinde Muller. Only in this treatment Siegfried was aware of his relationship to his innocent sister Sieglinde. Murnau wanted Lil Dagover, the popular German film star of the 1920s, for Sieglinde but she refused the part. Unable to cast it properly, the project was put aside as Pauline and Grover Cleveland Shapiro disappeared separately into the vast geography of America.

Five years later, Bella received a postcard from Pauline in Detroit. She stated that she had remarried and had a new family of her own; there was not a word asking about Seymour or Grover Cleveland, only the hope that Max and Bella were well. She signed it with her birth name, Rivka. More important, and more terrible for Bella, there was no return address. "Just as well," Bella told Max, "from now on I am Seymour Shelupsky's mother."

Max protested, "Bella, look where the first lie took us," but Bella replied that there was no good truth they could tell the growing boy that could cover his parentage. If Bella seemed a bit old for motherhood, the boy would never notice. The ghetto was filled with worn-looking women who carried infants in their arms. The true wonder of it was that no one, during

Bella and Max's long lifetime ever told Seymour Shapiro, now Shelupsky, the origins of his birth. In fact, Cousin Bella told me that he went to his death at age forty of a neuromuscular disorder still believing that Bella and Max were his parents. It had been noted by Max that the Rabbi had died shortly thereafter of a horrid skin cancer that ate his face after revealing Bella's secret to his reporter son. The reporter was killed in a subway derailment a few months later, or so Bella told me. It was clear to her that a sleeping God had finally awakened to punish anyone who tried to exploit her tragedy.

"Sorrow must be respected," so Cousin Bella told me. "No man should profit from it."

And as far as I knew, no man ever did.

A Christmas Lilly

For my young granddaughters,
Vivian, Zoe and Emily.

You have already inherited your great-grandmother's
beauty. May you also inherit her generous spirit and her
delicious home-made wisdom.

Lilly at fourteen in 1917

My mother's name was Lilly. She was a born escape artist. At three she escaped the murderous pogroms of Tsarist Russia, arriving at the Lower East Side of New York where her family of eight lived a desperate hand-to-mouth existence in a one room tenement on Hester Street. When her mother Sarah, her older sister Rebecca, and her brother Sam came down with the tuberculosis that eventually killed them, Lilly miraculously escaped that disease.

School had been Lilly's escape from the impoverished immigrant life that was destroying her family. School had taught her to speak English correctly, write with a lovely penmanship, and learn of life beyond the ghetto. The years before the First World War had seen one recession after another, and Lilly's father, my grandfather, a tailor by trade, was often unemployed. After her mother died, Lilly was obliged to leave school early to work towards paying for the care of her dying brother and sister in the Colorado sanitarium. There was only Lilly to supplement her father's meager income. But hard times do not necessarily make hard people. My mother escaped the callousness, and the bitterness that many poor children developed as armor against an indifferent, if not a cruel world.

Lilly escaped that ruinous bitterness because of Miss Emily Stokes, her last school teacher, a young African American. Miss Stokes, discovering that Lilly's mother had recently died, and that the girl would soon be obliged to leave school for work, hoped to keep the sad child from despair. The teacher gave Lilly a cloth doll at Christmas, one with a long calico two sided skirt that featured a white baby on one end and a black baby on the other. She would buy her promising student food for lunch so she was sure the child had one good meal. Because of Miss Stokes' kindness Lilly escaped the casual bigotry that so many European immigrants felt towards the children of former slaves.

Even as a child Lilly had a rare, luminous beauty. That beauty helped her to escape the sweat shops that swallowed so many poor girls alive. At fourteen, tall and slender, with large brown eyes set in a movie star's face, she bobbed her long black hair and became a fashion model in the new garment district of Manhattan.

My genial, joking, and temperamental father Nathan came from a similarly impoverished family.

He was put to work as a ten-year-old boy to help feed the six younger children, eventually owning his own business and achieving middle class comfort in the midst of the Great Depression. When I was little I once asked him what he did for fun as a child. He replied, "Son, when I was a boy they hadn't invented childhood, let alone fun."

I was seven years old in the Christmas of 1939 when my mother took my sister Simone and me downtown to see the decorated windows of the Fifth Avenue department stores. We were captured by the beauty of the Christmas trees with their glittering lights as we listened to the carolers near Rockefeller Center. I watched in wonder as my mother gave a bell ringing Salvation Army Santa a twenty dollar bill to help feed the hungry. In my child's mind it seemed that she was throwing a fortune down a fake chimney for people she didn't even know. She called it "helping out," never charity, when she gave cash and food to the needy; not only to her struggling family members but to any strangers down on their luck who crossed her path in those hard Depression times.

On the way home by taxi-cab that evening my mother stopped the cab, told the driver to wait, and impulsively bought a small, scrawny four foot Christmas tree from a shivering vendor. He wrapped it in burlap at her request so that it could not be seen for what it was by curious neighbors as she carried it into our house. I figured that my mother had bought the tree out of pity for the poor man who was making few sales that night, or perhaps she felt pity for the tree itself, a loser pine if ever there was one. She now had the cab driver take her to the local five and dime where she bought some silver tinsel, cellophane garlands, glass ornaments and peppermint candy canes. "All we need now is for it to snow tomorrow," my mother said as she smuggled the tree into our house.

My father was not at all religious but he questioned the propriety of that tree when he came home from his downtown office. "What's that bush doing here?" he asked. "It's for the children," my mother replied. He knew better than to argue with that. "For the children" was her final word, never to be disputed. She told him that Chanukah was taken care of; we had the brass menorah on the fireplace mantle whose candles she lit for the festival of lights, when she remembered to do so, but that was no reason to keep a Christmas tree out of her children's lives. As ever she made up her own rules as she went along, advising him that one thing had nothing to do with the other. The tree stayed.

Despite her defense of that paltry tree my mother hoped to keep it a secret from her pious older sister Ida who was troubled that Lilly had broken with the kosher dietary laws, and no longer observed the Sabbath. Lilly held a skeptical view of the Almighty; oh, she believed He was there alright, but for reasons she couldn't fathom God was off napping during her desperate childhood prayers, and certainly fast asleep in Europe in 1939. A few years earlier my mother had stopped keeping a kosher home when our pediatrician, the magisterial Dr. Herbert Jackson, advised her to introduce bacon strips and malted milkshakes into our everyday breakfast to add some flesh to the bones of her two skinny children. Ida protested that there were other ways to fatten up the children that would not offend God and Ida. Large bowls of lumpy oatmeal and teaspoons of cod-liver oil had kept her Gertrude plump and healthy. Mother, always merciful, chose to ignore Ida's breakfast menu. The sizzling, delicious bacon stayed in our diet, topping our French toast in warm maple syrup and melted butter.

Christmas morning arrived with a light snowfall as if by my mother's command. We children got up early and raced into the living room, dazzled by the decorated tree, all its spindly faults concealed by the garlands of glitter, tinsel, gold and silver glass ornaments, and the many wrapped gifts my mother had placed under it. I had received the new wooden fort and the cavalry of painted French Legionnaire soldiers I longed for, and my sister Simone had not one, but two Shirley Temple dolls. My mother confessed that she was unable to decide between the everyday Shirley and the Shirley dressed for a fancy ball, so she bought both for her young daughter. But more important to her were the books she bought for us. She had taught us to read early by first reading aloud to us and every so often pointing out the words on the page, and later by making up flash-cards on cut up shirt cardboards with new words printed in block letters for us to recognize. It worked. My smart sister read at four, and I trailed behind her lazily, reading at six.

There was a motivational book, Young Mozart, for my sister, who was often found struggling with her five finger exercises on our baby grand piano. There were two Jerry Todd books for me, juvenile novels, hugely popular at that time, which allowed a city boy to imagine that he lived in a small town with a gang of loyal friends who had exciting yet comical adventures. And there was "Treasure Island" in the brilliantly illustrated N.C. Wyeth edition, promising me days of escape with young Jim Hawkins in a world of pirates, mutiny, and buried treasure.

Into this scene of torn wrappings and cries of joy came an ominous ringing, someone with a heavy finger was pressing it hard against our doorbell.

Lilly knew at once that it was her older sister Ida accompanied by Ida's young daughter Gertrude, standing outside impatiently in the now heavily falling snow. Ida had brought Gertrude over to our house to play with my sister during this school holiday. It had been arranged on the telephone days before, and forgotten by my mother in the excitement of getting the children's gifts wrapped and the tree set up for Christmas.

My mother loved her homely, old fashioned sister, who had awkwardly but dutifully stepped into the role of mother for her during Lilly's bleak childhood. But she knew that Ida would be shocked, more likely horrified by the Christmas tree. It would be another sign of Lilly, "the American one," drifting away from the customs of their forefathers. In this time of murderous crimes against the Jews in Europe, and everyday nasty anti-Semitism in America, my mother didn't want to be regarded of as one who rejected her own people in their time of trial.

Lilly, who was always calm, suddenly panicked at the sound of that persistent doorbell. She didn't want a confrontation or even a conversation about that tree with her disapproving sister. She hastily picked up the tree, embracing it as she might a child to be rescued from a raging fire, and rushed towards the hall bathroom as pine needles, glittering garlands, and a fragile glass ornament fell and scattered in her wake. Hiding the tree safely inside the bathtub – its banishment was to last only as long as the visitors stayed – she closed the shower curtains concealing it from view. Only then did she answer the front door.

Ida stood there in the cold complaining that they had been forced to wait so long in the freezing snow that her Gertrude risked frost bite and pneumonia. My mother, who had a wonderful way of ignoring such complaints, praised ten year old Gertrude on her healthy complexion and her thick brown curls as the glum child removed her wet woolen stocking cap and gloves. Snow on coats was hastily shaken off outside. When Ida went to hang their coats in the nearby hall bathroom, the customary place for wet outdoor clothing, Lilly told her sister to hang them on the wall hooks nearby, so that the steam radiator would dry them. Another close escape. Galoshes were carefully placed on the inside doormat by our visitors to show their respect for my mother's spotless carpets and in homage to our gleaming hall linoleum scrubbed to a high shine with Murphy's Oil Soap. Ida was known to say that "you could eat off Lilly's floors," her highest compliment about my mother's housekeeping.

Mother offered Ida a cup of hot tea to take off the chill with a slice of marble pound cake, but Ida, as ever, refused; you might be able to eat off Lilly's floors but not her china. God alone knew if there was bacon fat clinging to our tea-cups and pork rinds concealed in the Drake's cake.

Ida entered the living room and delivered a noisy wet kiss on my warm cheek and one for my sister which we wiped off discreetly with the sleeves of our bathrobes. I whispered to my sister that thanks to Aunt Ida's kisses we wouldn't have to bathe for a week. Ida then surveyed the Christmas stockings hanging from the mantle stuffed with candies, crayons, miniature playing cards, wooden spinning tops, jacks and little mesh bags of marbles; the trinket laden stockings that my mother had forgotten to remove in her haste to hide the tree. The stockings seemed to evade Ida's scrutiny and it appeared that my mother would entirely escape censure today, thanks to the menorah which acted as her shield of righteousness. Lilly now gave Gertrude a new Nancy Drew book she had bought for her niece's Chanukah gift. Gertrude looked at it sadly and said, "Thank you Aunt Lilly but I read this one already. Give it to Simone."

Ida glanced at the new toys that littered our living room floor and fired her first round of armor-piercing questions, "Lilly, what is this? A toy shop? Don't you know that you're spoiling your children?"

My aunt continued to condemn her younger sister's child-rearing methods, contrasting them with her own superior mothering. "Gertrude only gets one doll a year, and that's on her birthday, and she's so careful with that doll you'd think it was never played with. She's not spoiled. I could give her more, we did okay this year, but I won't spoil her. You give them too much. You love them too much. You make them too happy. You're spoiling them rotten."

My mother now reached the limits of her patience. This was one argument she could not escape. She replied that her children were not spoiled, trying hard not to show the great annoyance that she felt.

"Ida, we were spoiled. We had nothing, and there's nothing like nothing for spoiling children. Toys don't do that, and happiness doesn't do that. And love certainly doesn't do that."

Soon the evidence was piling up before Ida on the floor, that incriminating trail of tinsel, the suspicious scattering of pine needles, and the tell-tale shards of gleaming colored glass from a broken ornament on the Persian rug.

"Do you have a Christmas tree here, Lilly?"

Knowing that the game was up my mother calmly replied, "Yes, there's one growing in the hall bathtub. Go look. I've got a real pine forest in there."

"You wouldn't?" Ida protested.

"I would. And I did," my mother said, refusing to apologize for her frail tree. She had not risen from the depths of that ghetto on her beauty and her smile alone. Lilly's loving nature was tempered by a will of iron, and when challenged she could stand up to anyone, even her older sister, the hanging judge. If Ida was going to make a fuss over this Christmas tree Lilly would not back down. For my mother the eleventh commandment was "mind thy own business."

Ida started towards the bathroom to see that odious tree but was stopped by Gertrude's sudden cry of dismay. The child had seen the two Shirley Temple dolls cradled in their packaging amidst the torn Christmas wrappings. "It isn't fair," Gertrude lamented. "It isn't fair."

"No it isn't," my mother agreed. "Simone, please give Gertrude one of your dolls."

When my sister protested, tears forming in her eyes, ready to match Gertie sob for sob in any misery competition my mother said something that I have never forgotten.

"I know. Sometimes it's hard to be kind. But it's just like playing the piano. It gets easier with practice."

My sister picked up the doll in the modest polka dot cotton dress and reluctantly handed it over to her anguished cousin, keeping the Shirley in the fancy chiffon ball-gown for herself. There are limits to any child's generosity. Two of my toy soldiers, Corsairs on horseback with ingenious, removable sabers, were thrown in with the doll when the insatiable Gertrude eyed them longingly, despite my protest that I needed them to fight for the French Foreign Legion. Satisfied at last, Gertrude stopped her insidious and very productive crying. A smile of triumph appeared on her thin lips for these acts of generosity imposed upon her younger cousins by our mother. Soon, we were on the floor playing together, all resentment dissipated; even Ida relaxed, sat down in a club chair, and graciously accepted a glass of tap water as she began to complain about our other relatives.

I believe my mother got back as much as she gave to us that Christmas. My bright, sparkling sister filled the house with mischief and laughter, and needy, nervy me was always good for a wisecrack that made her smile. We were Lily's protection against a cruel past which threatened to break through like a flood, bringing with it the debris of those old childhood sorrows. Christmas was also a time to recall Miss Stokes munificent gift of that double sided doll. I suppose my mother was surprised by our protests when she made us share our gifts with Cousin Gertrude. Generosity was as natural for her as breathing and loving. Now, whenever the holiday come around, I think of my mother Lilly, long gone, with her great smile, her generous heart, her spindly Christmas tree, and her talent for kindness which never needed practice.

Sherman Yellen, playwright, librettist, screenwriter, lyricist and now memoirist, was nominated for a Tony Award for his book for the 1970 musical *The Rothschilds*, with a score by *Fiddler on the Roof* songwriters Jerry Bock and Sheldon Harnick. Sherman wrote the libretto for the Will Holt and Gary William Freidman musical *Treasure*  *Island*, winner of the Broadway World Best Regional musical Award (2012). Among his many theater works is his satirical sketch "Delicious Indignities" which appeared in the New York and London revue *Oh! Calcutta!* His straight plays on and off Broadway include *New Gods for Lovers*, *Strangers*, and *December Fools*.

Sherman was librettist and lyricist for *Josephine Tonight*, an original musical he wrote with the late composer Wally Harper about the early life of Josephine Baker, which *The Chicago Sun-Times* called "a shining new musical" and which the DC press praised for being "so hot that it sizzles."

In his youth he worked as a librettist with legendary composer Richard Rodgers. Together with Sheldon Harnick they recently revised the Rodgers-Harnick musical *Rex* about Henry VIII. This new version had a successful premiere in Toronto.

His teleplays have won him two Emmy Awards and a Peabody Award, first for his *John Adams, Lawyer* in the PBS series *The Adams Chronicles*, and later for *An Early Frost*, a groundbreaking drama about AIDS in America broadcast on NBC, as well as an Emmy Nomination for his *Hallmark Hall of Fame* version of *Beauty and the Beast* starring George C. Scott. Sherman's screenplay adaptations of classic novels range from *Great Expectations* to *Phantom of the Opera*. He has received awards in Arts and Letters from Bard College, and he is a frequent contributor of essays on the arts, literature, and politics to online publications such as *The Huffington Post*.

In recent years, Sherman has devoted much of his time to his memoir *Spotless*, a recreation of his New York childhood in the 1930s and '40s and his young adulthood in the 1950s, which will be published later this year.

Sherman is married, the father of two sons, Nicholas and Christopher, and has three much loved granddaughters. He has lived in London and Los Angeles, worked in Berlin and Budapest, but home was, is, and always will be New York City.

Also Recommended

The Flash of Midnight
By Robert Armin

Taking its inspiration from Voltaire's *Candide*, Robert Armin's novel *The Flash of Midnight* recounts the bisexual escapades of Laurie Norber, a young woman who steadfastly believes that true love is just around the corner, never imagining that in June of 1969 she will become the spark that ignites a sexual revolution at a Greenwich Village bar called the Stonewall Inn.

Trade Paperback ISBN-10: 1463508077 **ISBN-13:** 978-1463508074
Also Available in **Kindle eBook** and **Unabridged Audiobook**

MORECLACKE **PUBLISHING**

Made in the USA
Charleston, SC
24 February 2015